This book belongs to:

To Langston,
Thank you for listening to me read and letting me hold Pickles!
With Love, Diana Lee ♡

"Mommy, Mommy," DLee cries.

"I cannot sleep! I am afraid of the eyes!"

"I do not see any eyes," her mommy said,

after rushing to the foot of her bed.

"The eyes in my closet, Mommy!

The big blue eyes!"

"They are right over there,"

she quickly replies.

Her mommy looks at the closet

but she sees nothing there.

Could the eyes have disappeared

leaving the closet bare?

DLee is confused.

"I think you were imagining those blues!"

Mommy said, amused.

"Mommy, Mommy! The monster was there!"

"It had blue eyes, and pink and purple hair!"

"It was a monster!" she screamed.

"And it was as large as a bear!"

"Okay! Okay! Let me turn on the light."

"I am sure it was nothing more than just a fright."

Mommy turns on the light in a flash.

Then out jumps DLee's cat

wearing a pink and purple sash.

"Mr. Mustache, it is you! You silly little cat!"

"How did you end up in my closet wearing that?"

"You see, DLee, there are no monsters in here."

"There are no such things as monsters, my dear."

"So dry your eyes and get into bed."

"Monsters are not real," Mommy quickly said.

"Next time you feel scared,

be sure to remember this."

Then her mommy gave DLee a big hug

and a huge kiss.

"Now lie down and close each eye."

"I'll see you in the morning,

my little pumpkin pie."

"Sleep tight…"

And DLee drifted off without even

saying goodnight.

If you liked this book, check out DLee in:

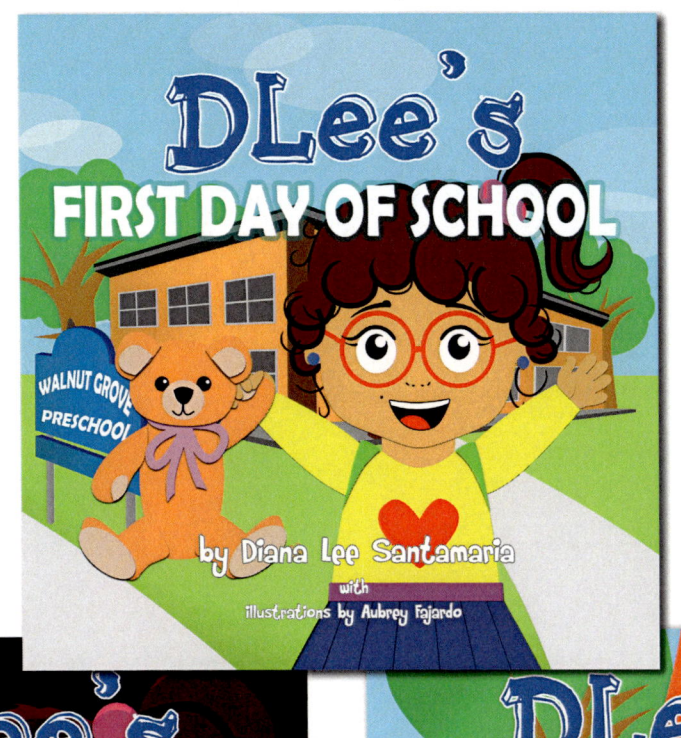

www.dleesworld.com

COPYRIGHT © 2014 DLEE'S WORLD, LLC.
ALL RIGHTS RESERVED.

Made in the USA
Middletown, DE
07 January 2016